Easter and Spring Crafting With Reny:
40 easy paper projects for children

by Mgr. Renata Kolibova. All rights reserved.

Published in 2020 by Mgr. Kolibova Renata, Olomoucka 2, Brno 618 00, Czechia.

Printed via Amazon Kindle Direct Publishing, for more details, see last page of the book.

First Edition

ISBN 978-80-907605-1-6

www.craftingwithreny.com

SPRING AND EASTER

PAPER CRAFTING with Reny

BY RENATA KOLIBOVA

DEDICATION

TO MY DAUGHTER ELISKA, WHO IS ON ALL PICTURES WITH ME.

WELCOME TO THE WORLD.

MOM

Foreword

Welcome to the series of craft books, "Crafting with Reny" this is my 3rd book and I very excited to share new ideas with you.

This book will set you up for spring and Easter crafting activities with 40 beautiful and simple paper crafts with super clear-illustrated instructions.

I'm combining my years of experience as a kindergarten teacher and over 1000 crafts I've shared online, to convince you that crafting is easy and fun to do!

When you finish this book, you'll not only have created a beautiful home or school decorations but also lovely gift cards for Easter holidays. I am sure you will enjoy them with your loved ones.

Happy Easter!

Who's Reny?

I'm a kindergarten teacher and have been a craft blogger since 2015, making paper craft videos and tutorials.

I'm followed by millions of teachers and parents just like yourself from all around the globe.

Email me for *free* coloring templates!

Everyone loves freebies, right? :) I have prepared for you 40 coloring templates from my first book in one PDF file, ready for printing.

You can use them at home or make copies for your class or any activities with children.

Just email me and I will send you a copy with my sincere thanks for getting this book :)

My email is:
craftingwithreny@gmail.com

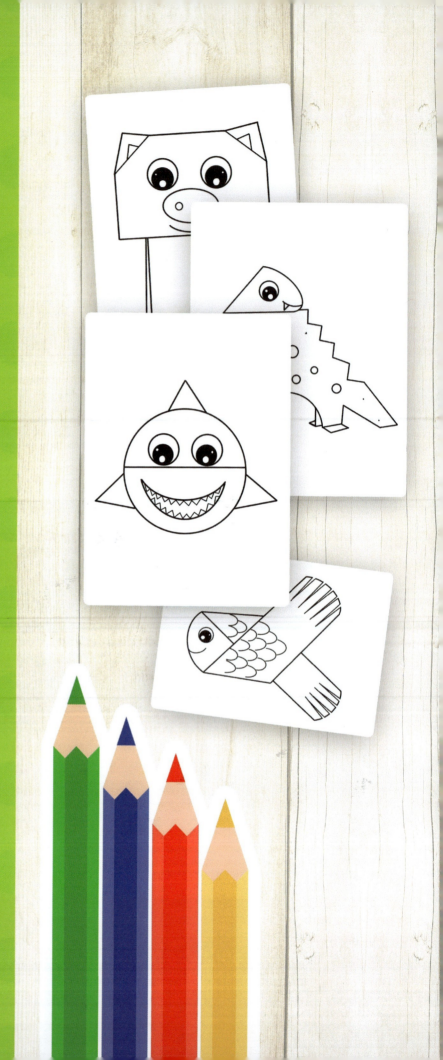

Tips & Tricks

Here are quick instructions to make funny eyes.

The next pages will cover shapes and dimensions for all the crafts in the book.

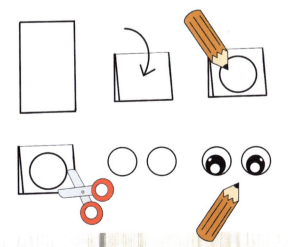

Tips for making circles

A4
210 × 297 mm
Any sheet thickness

or

Letter
8.5 × 11 in
Any sheet thickness

200 × 200 mm
8 × 8 inch

65 × 65 mm
2.5 × 2.5 inch

Tips for making strips

A4
210 × 297 mm

Any sheet thickness

Or

Letter
8.5 × 11 in

Any sheet thickness

1/2 of A4 or Letter

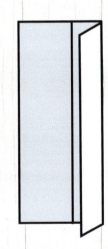

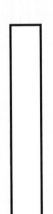

1/4 of A4 or Letter

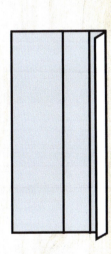

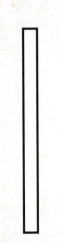

1/8 of A4 or Letter

SPRING CRAFTS

Ladybug	10	Tulip patch	20
Snail	11	Hyacinth	21
Bird nest	12	Flower hearth	22
Bird	13	Flower	23
Caterpillar	14	Tulip	24
Ant	15	Sun	25
Caterpillar	16	Frog	26
Dragonfly	17	Bee	27
Watering can	18	Stork	28
Carrot	19	Butterfly	29

Ladybug

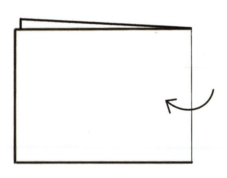
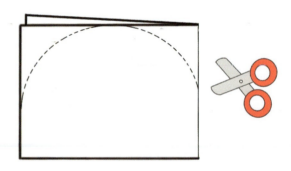
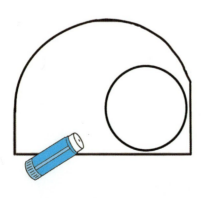
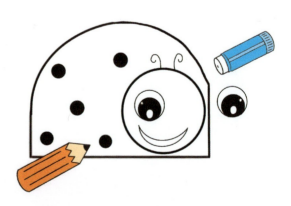

Snail

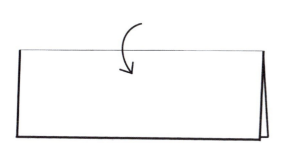
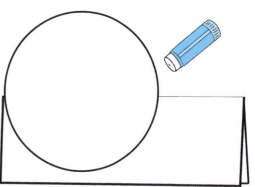
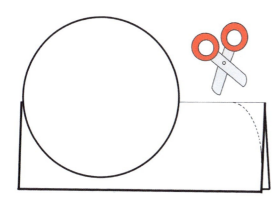

Bird nest

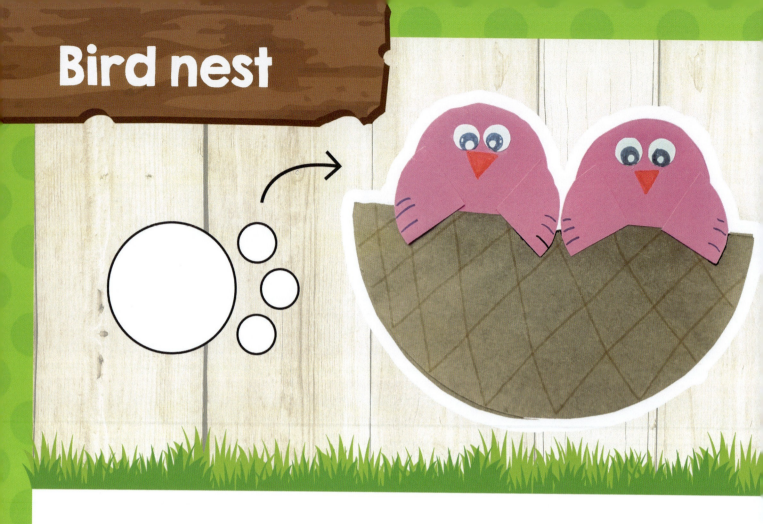
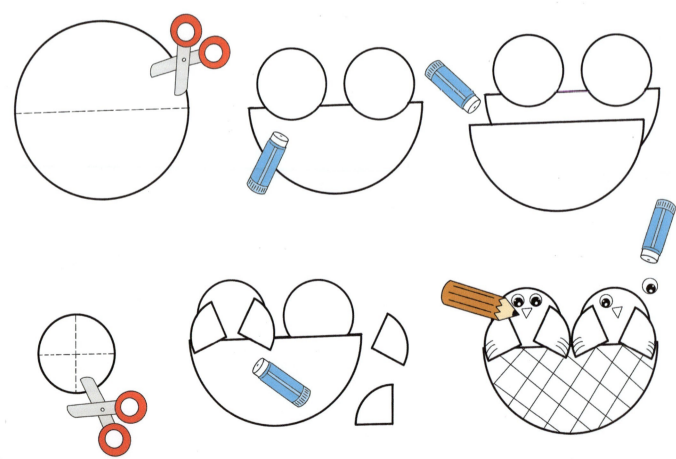

Bird

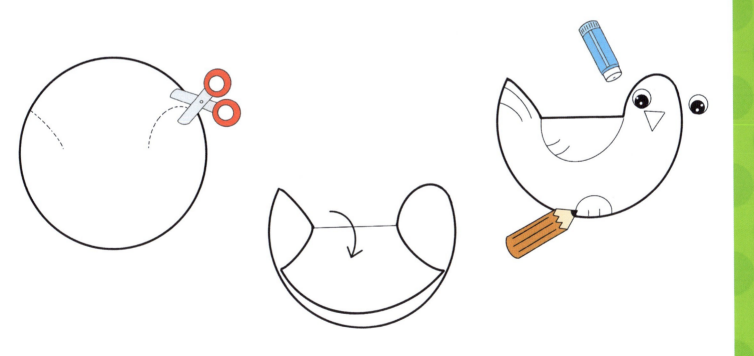

Caterpillar

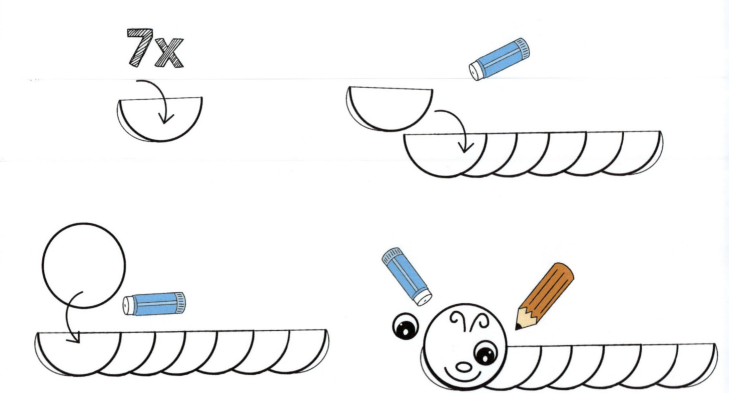

Ant

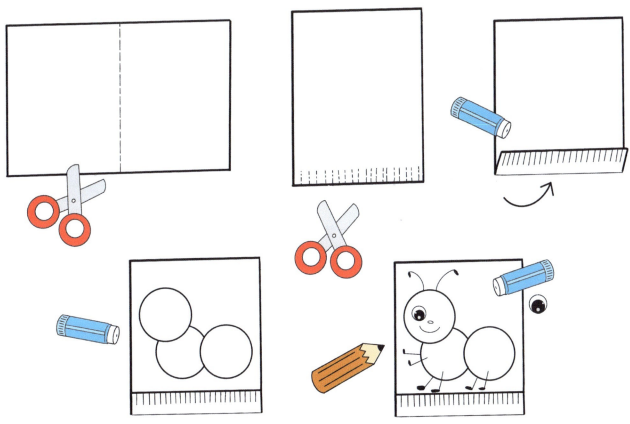

Caterpillar

Dragonfly

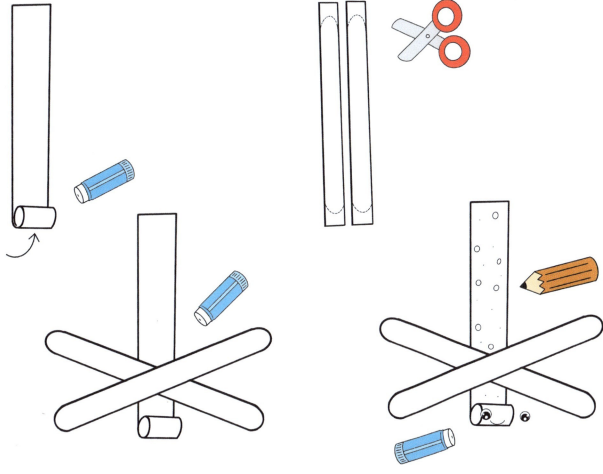

17

Watering can

Carrot

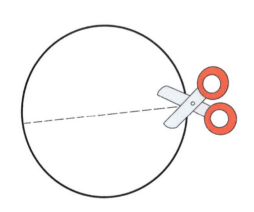
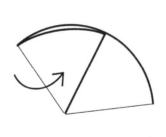

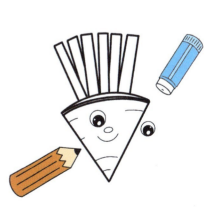

19

Tulip patch

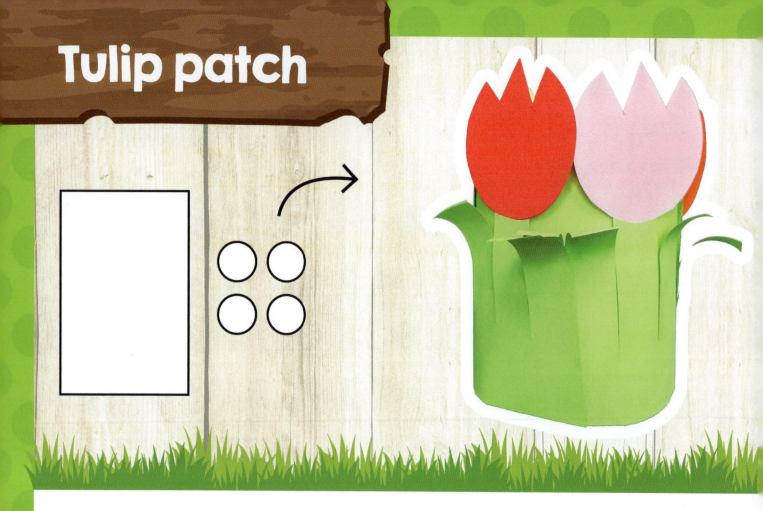
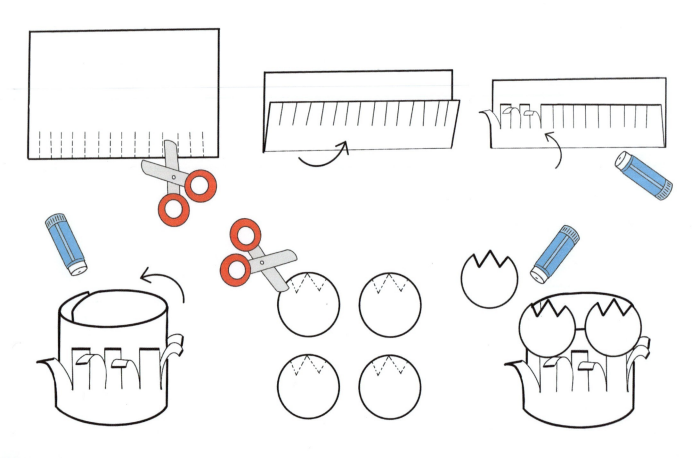

20

Hyacinth

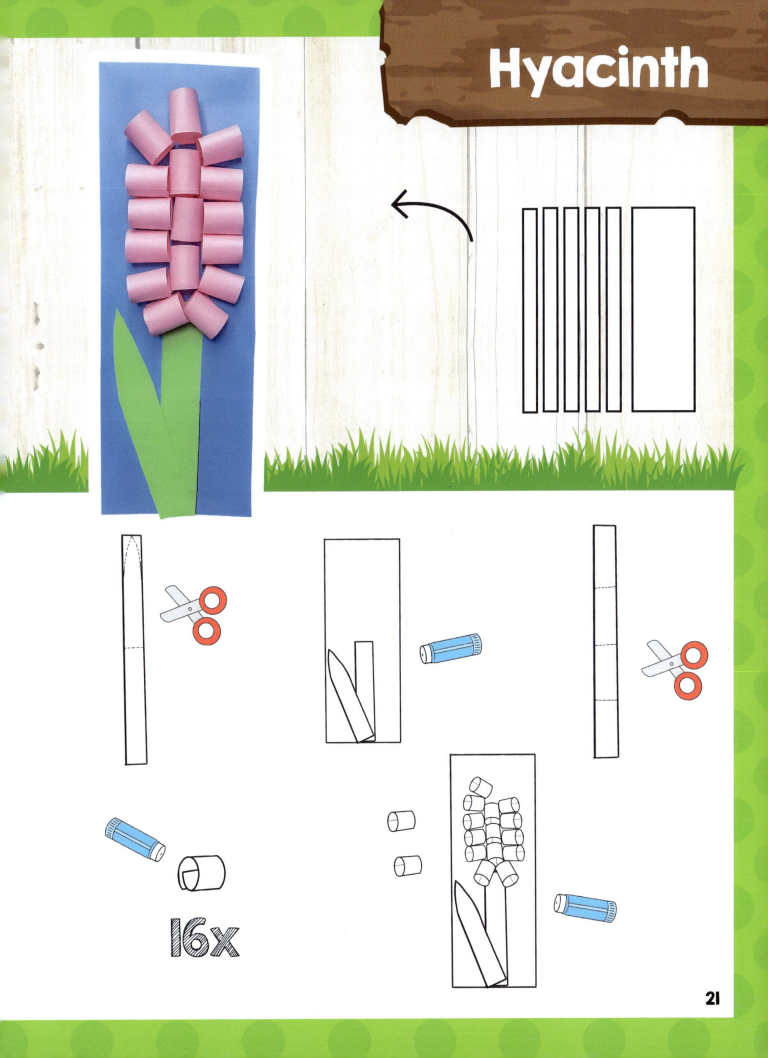

16x

Flower hearth

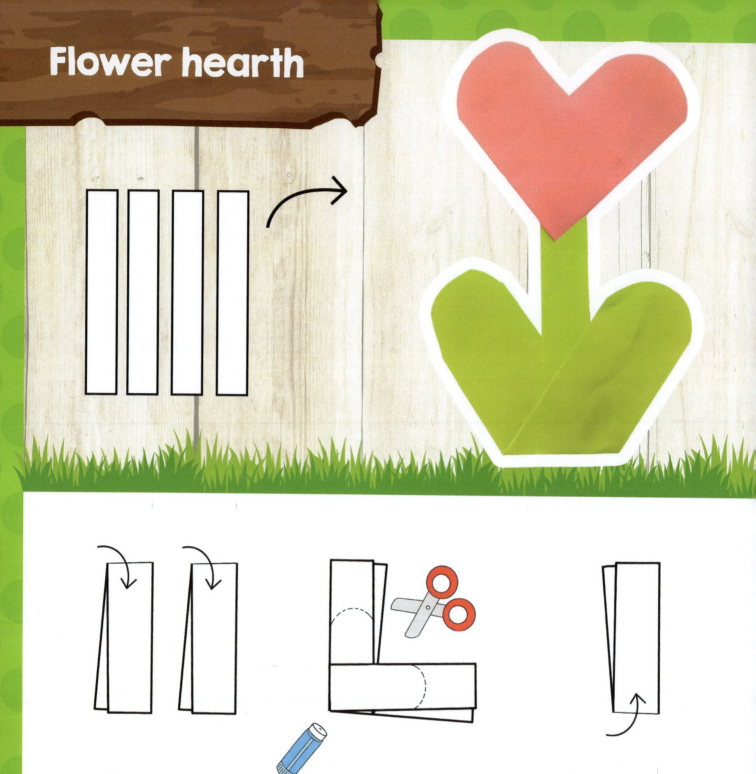
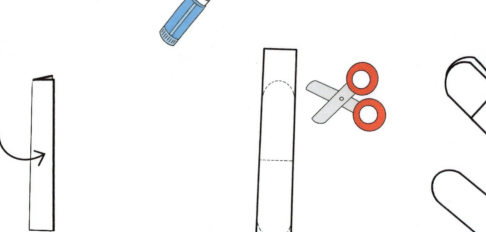

Flower

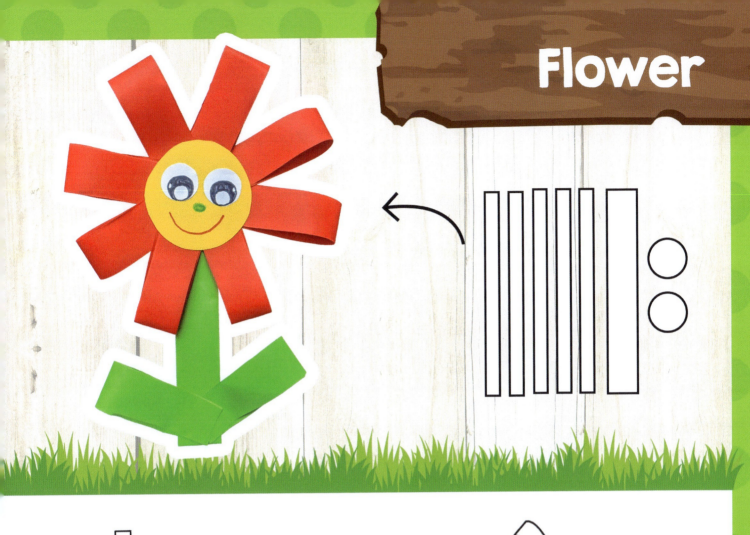

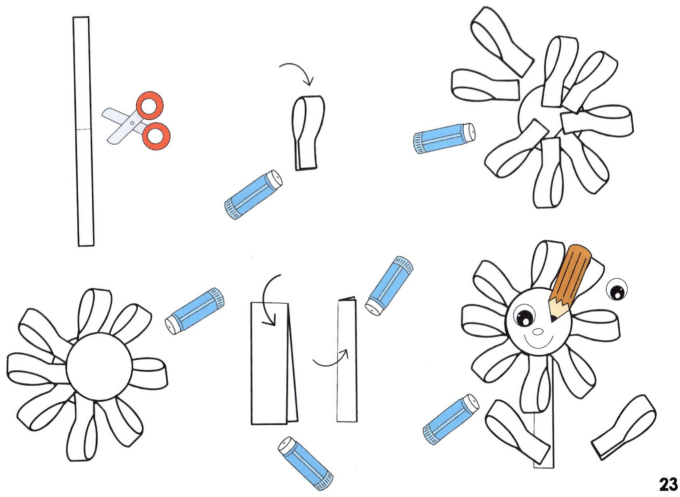

23

Tulip

Sun

14x

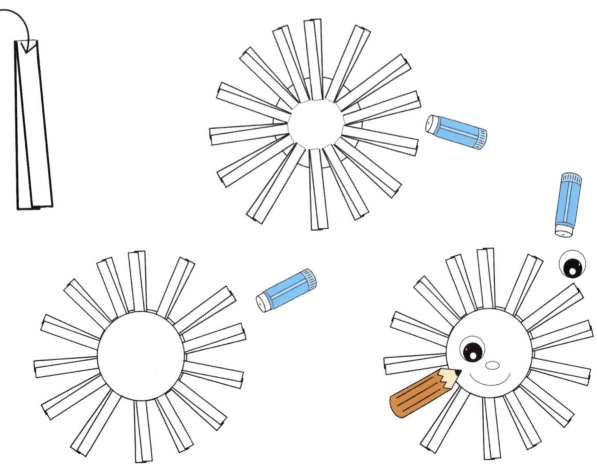

Frog

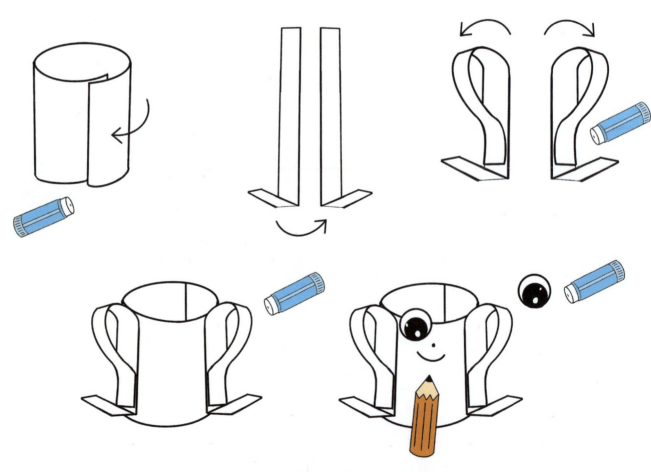

26

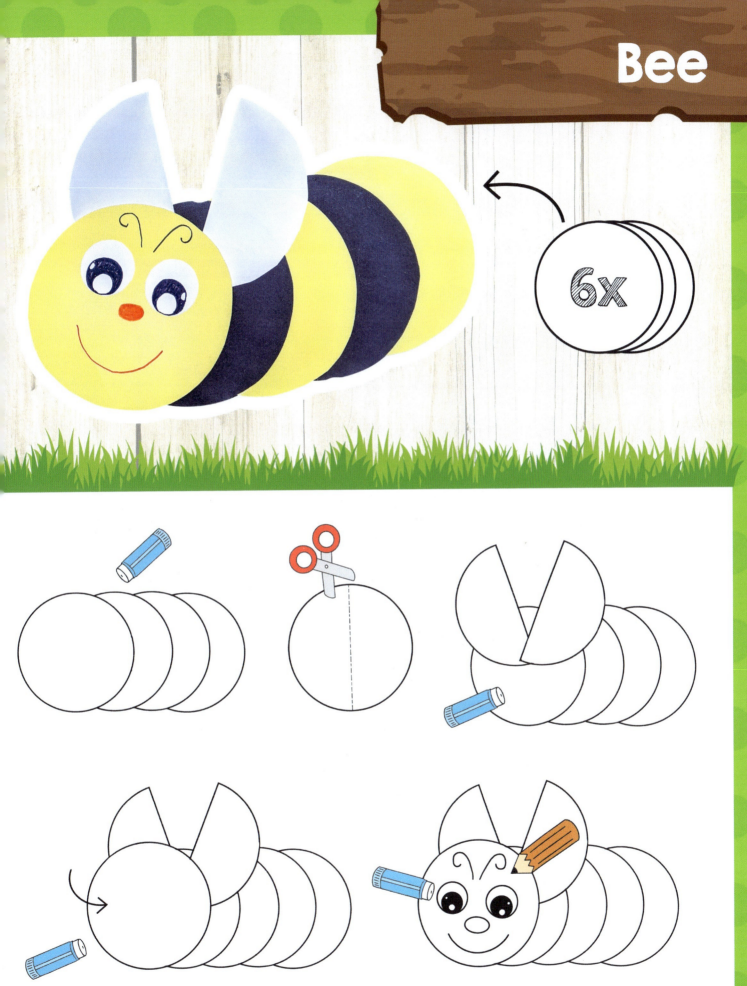

Stork

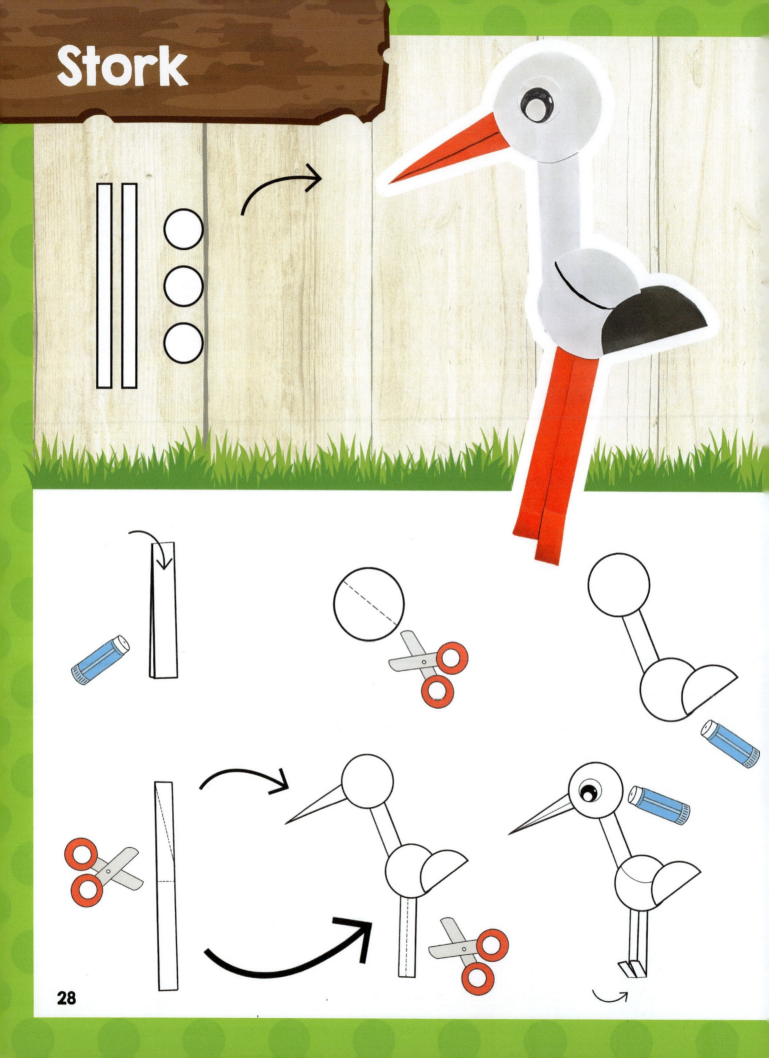

Butterfly

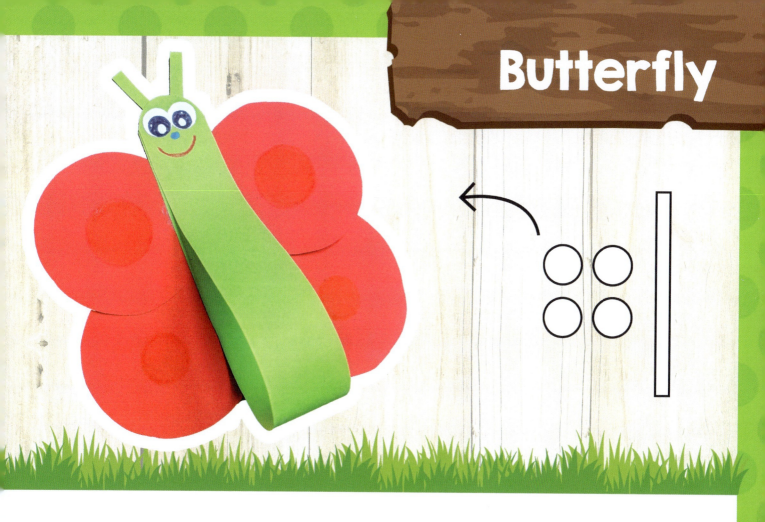
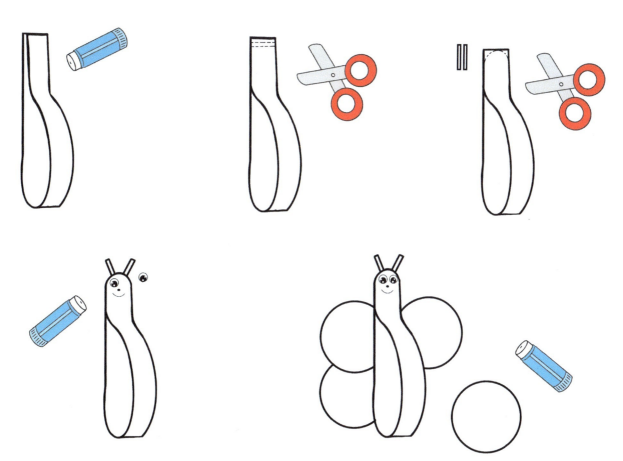

29

EASTER CRAFTS

Duckling	32	Bunny	42
Rabbit	33	Sheep	43
Basket	34	Easter eggs	44
Rooster	35	Duckling	45
Chicken card	36	Easter wreath	46
White hen	37	Rabbit	47
Brown hen	38	Chicken card	48
Chick	39	Egg card	49
Chicken	40	Bunny card	50
Sheep	41	Easter card	51

Rabbit

Basket

Rooster

Chicken card

White hen

Chick

Sheep

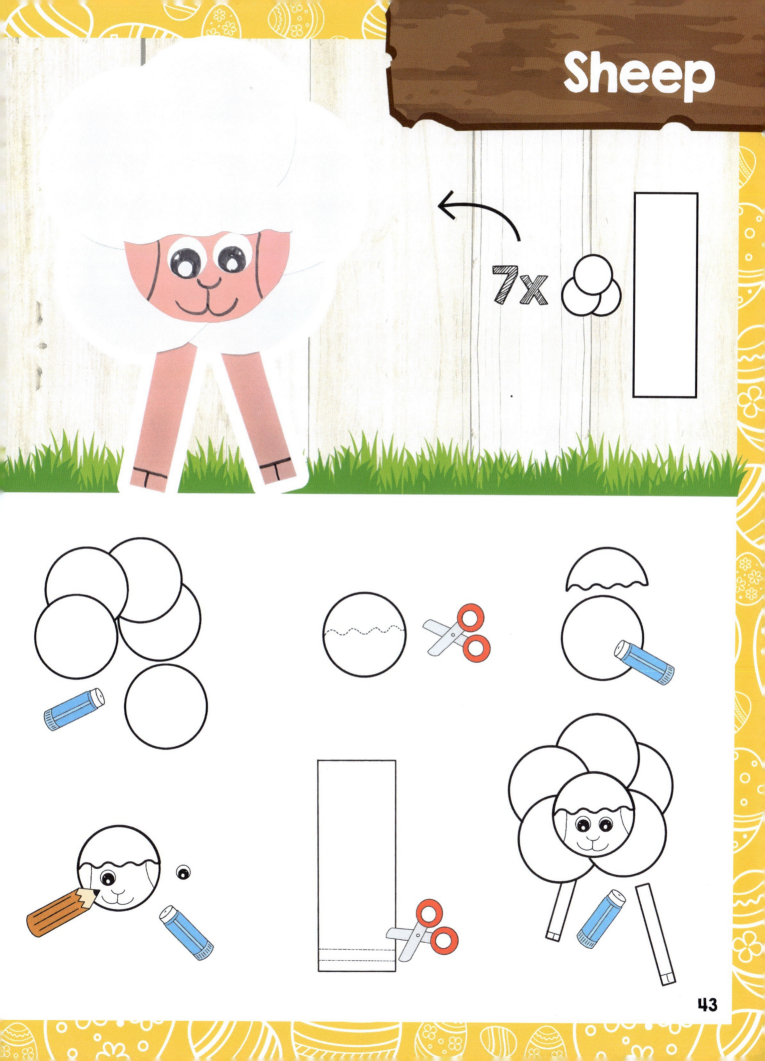

Sheep

7x

Easter egg

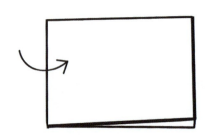

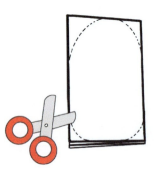

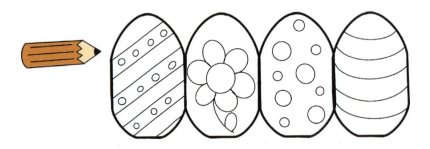

Duckling

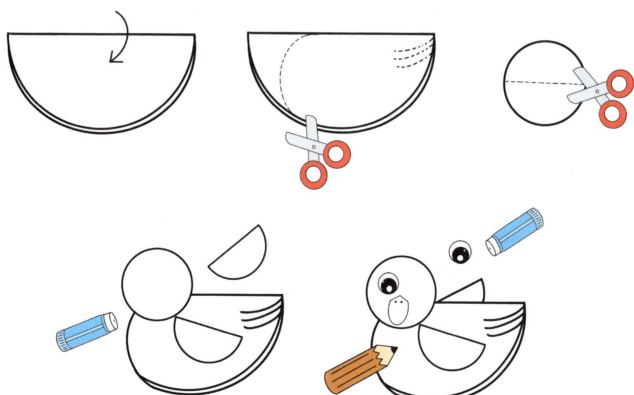

45

Easter wreath

Rabbit

Egg card

Bunny card

Printed in Poland
by Amazon Fulfillment
Poland Sp. z o.o., Wrocław